Welcome to

Pawnee

The Ultimate Fan's Guide to
PARKS AND RECREATION

AMY LEWIS

Smith
Street
Books

The first season of *Parks and Recreation* hit our screens in 2009, introducing us to the inner workings of the Pawnee Parks and Recreation Department. Created by Greg Daniels and Michael Schur, the show was produced by Amy Poehler, who played the central character, Leslie Knope. Shot in a mockumentary style, we meet Leslie, the passionate Deputy Director and workaholic who loves Pawnee so much that she will go to almost any length to help. We are also introduced to Knope's considerably less enthusiastic co-workers: Ron Swanson, the gruff no-nonsense head of the department and his mostly apathetic team of Mark, April, Tom, Donna and Jerry.

In 2008 Greg Daniels had experienced huge success with *The Office* and was looking to follow up with a new project at NBC. The concept was similar in some ways to its predecessor, particularly the mockumentary format and the use of improvisation. Initially, there were parallels drawn by critics between the characters Michael Scott and Leslie Knope. However, while the earlier seasons focussed on Knope's unpopularity and fumbles, her character would develop into a loved and respected member of her team – an accolade that Michael Scott never fully achieved.

Parks and Recreation received several awards and was nominated for 14 Prime Time Emmys. Amy Poehler won a Golden Globe for her performance, and the show was nominated for a Golden Globe for Best Television Series – Musical or Comedy. In addition to the show's critical success, *Parks and Recreation* is currently one of the most watched shows on Netflix, a decade after it began. The fact that the show puts friendship and hard work at its core, along with humor, physical comedy, warmth and positivity, means that *Parks and Recreation* is loved by audiences of all ages around the world.

Hi, I'm Leslie Knope and I am proud to represent the great city of Pawnee. Today I want to share my vision with you all. Sure, we do things a little different here in Pawnee. And yes, people put their whole mouths over the drinking fountain. But Pawnee is the best city in Indiana, maybe America and possibly the world. And I wouldn't want to live anywhere else.

In Pawnee we've got the perfect blend of commerce and nature. Take a stroll down Main Street and enjoy breakfast all day at JJ's Diner, or perhaps a dinosaur-themed meal cooked "medium roar" at Jurassic Fork. But it's not just fine dining in Pawnee. We've got the less discerning customers' needs covered at Paunch Burger, Big-N-Wide, Fat Sack – and don't forget Colonel Plump's Slop Trough.

Walk into Pawnee City Hall and you are sure to be greeted with a smile. Head up to the Parks and Recreation Department and one of our team will be more than willing to suggest a place for you to go take a hike. On your journey you may even pass by our official city tree, the Indiana Common Shrub. But watch out for raccoons. If they get too close you've gotta hiss at them. It's the only language they understand.

If you hike too far and get to Eagleton, turn back. Eagleton sucks. They might have better schools, cleaner sidewalks and impossibly straight teeth. But they don't have hearts.

I've written this acronym for Pawnee, and hope to have it displayed on a sign as our visitors drive into town:

P eople helping people to succeed
A ll the waffles you can eat
W omen getting things done
N ative American people are now allowed in our hospitals
E leventh ranking team in Southern Indiana High School Basketball
E agleton is the worst city

The Pawnee motto states: First in friendship, Fourth in Obesity. And I, Leslie Knope, truly believe that together we can beat obese children ... wait, that came out wrong.

SEASON ONE

The first season, made up of just six episodes, is centered around an abandoned pit in the town (Lot 48), which Leslie makes her passion project, wanting to turn it into a park for the townspeople. Leslie meets Ann, who lives next door to the pit and is dating Andy, an unemployed musician for a band he claims to be "Matchbox Twenty meets The Fray." Andy has broken both of his legs falling into the abandoned pit and is living on his girlfriend Ann's couch, where she feeds and cleans up after him while working full time as a nurse at the local hospital.

Leslie has a crush on city planner Mark. However, her affections are not returned, and he shows more interest in Ann. Despite this, Leslie decides to make Ann her new best friend. They attend a government function together and Ann is mistaken for Leslie's partner due to Leslie's tuxedo, and masculine haircut courtesy of the local Pawnee barber.

Under the questionable influence of her mother, Marlene, an important official in the Pawnee school system, Leslie attempts to bribe a government official and is tricked into going on a date with a far older man because he has influence on zoning permits. The season ends with Andy's band playing at a local bar. Tom is busy showing off his attractive wife, Wendy, while Ann and Andy's relationship is in jeopardy after it turns out he should have had his leg casts removed weeks ago but was enjoying Ann's doting on him.

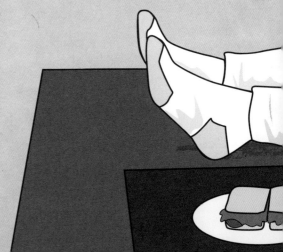

The critical response to the first season was mixed, with many finding it too similar to NBC's highly successful *The Office*. Notably, in these early episodes, people in the Parks Department are very critical of Leslie and she is the butt of many jokes. The show takes a far more positive turn in future seasons, with people in the department growing closer and celebrating each other's wins. This positivity and comradery amongst the characters was arguably key to the increasing popularity of *Parks and Recreation* with audiences.

BUTTER CHIPS

The Cast →

Through the show's seven-season run, one of its true joys was the quality of the cast, many of who were from stand-up and improv backgrounds, as well as notable shows like *Saturday Night Live*. After the first season, the critical and popular success of *Parks and Recreation* landed some very high profile cameos and recurring guest appearances from famous comics, film stars and even some senior members of the US government who would make their acting debuts.

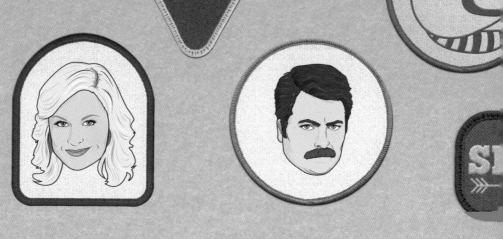

Amy Poehler (Leslie Knope)

Amy Poehler's career is one that most comedians could only dream of. After starting her improv career at the infamous Second City in Chicago in the 90s, she became a highly popular cast member of *Saturday Night Live* in the 2000s alongside her friend and collaborator Tina Fey. In 2001 Poehler set up her own all-female production company called Paper Kite Productions, before she joined *Parks and Recreation* as the star and producer. Along with Natasha Lyonne and Leslye Headland, she wrote and was executive producer on the critically acclaimed comedy-drama series *Russian Doll* (2019). Poehler also founded the Smart Girls organization along with Meredith Walker, which is dedicated to helping young people cultivate their authentic selves. She has also written a memoir entitled *Yes Please* (2014).

Nick Offerman (Ron Swanson)

Offerman is best known to most of us as Ron Swanson, however he had already made his mark in theater before joining the show. He initially met Amy Poehler in Chicago in the 90s and was also a guest star on his wife, Megan Mullally's hit show *Will & Grace* before taking on the role of Ron. He has also starred in films, including *Miss Congeniality 2: Armed and Fabulous* (2005), *Sin City* (2005) and *The Men Who Stare at Goats* (2009). He toured the USA in 2019 with his comedy show *All Rise*, a successful follow-up to his 2017 Full Bush tour. Arguably the most popular character on the show, Offerman shares his love of carpentry with Ron Swanson and currently hosts a show about crafting, alongside Amy Poehler, called *Making It* (2018–), where contestants compete to craft items out of "unexpected materials."

Rashida Jones (Ann Perkins)

Fans of NBC's *The Office* would recognize Rashida Jones as Jim's other love interest, Karen Filippelli. A Harvard graduate, Jones is also known for her famous father, Quincy Jones. In 2018 her documentary *Quincy*, about her father was shown on Netflix, winning a Grammy Award for Best Music Film in 2019. Jones has starred in such films as *I Love You, Man* (2009), *The Social Network* (2010) and *Our Idiot Brother* (2011). A passionate Democrat, Jones has publicly campaigned for the last four Democratic presidential candidates.

Chris Pratt (Andy Dwyer)

Parks and Recreation was arguably Chris Pratt's break-out role. In a parallel with his character Andy, Pratt never finished college and was once homeless, living in Maui, sleeping in a van and a tent on the beach. While filming the show, Pratt had roles in *The Lego Movie* (2014) and *Guardians of the Galaxy* (2014). Pratt was offered the lead role in *Jurassic World* in 2015, which resulted in a significant body transformation for Pratt – this is obvious in the later seasons of *Parks and Recreation*. In 2015, *Time* named Pratt in their Time 100 list as one of the 100 most influential people in the world.

Aubrey Plaza (April Ludgate)

Aubrey Plaza began her career performing improv and sketch comedy with the Upright Citizens Brigade Theatre in New York City. Much like her character April, Plaza has worked in many intern jobs, including at NBC. Her real-life glib outlook and deadpan delivery matches April's, which has earned her a cult following among fans. She appeared in *Funny People* (2009) and *Scott Pilgrim vs. the World* (2010), had her first leading role as Darius Britt in the comedy *Safety Not Guaranteed* (2012), and starred in *Child's Play* (2019).

Adam Scott (Ben Wyatt)

Adam Scott came to *Parks and Recreation* with significant television experience under his belt. Comfortable in both comedic and serious roles, he played Griff Hawkins in the series *Boy Meets World*, Josh in *Party of Five* and had a guest role on *Six Feet Under*. He was also in the first and second seasons of *Eastbound & Down*. From 2009 to 2010 he appeared on the sitcom *Party Down*. His feature films include *The Aviator* (2004), *Knocked Up* (2007) and *Leap Year* (2010), and he starred in the critically acclaimed series *Big Little Lies*. Adam Scott married Naomi Sablan in 2005 and they have two children together.

Retta (Donna Meagle)

After graduating from college, Retta (Marietta Sangai Sirleaf) worked as a chemist while performing stand-up at Charlie Goodnights Comedy Club in North Carolina. Eventually she moved to Los Angeles to pursue her comedy career. Retta scored roles in the highly successful television comedies *It's Always Sunny in Philadelphia*, *Drunk History* and *Key & Peele*. In 2018, Retta published a series of essays in a book called *So Close to Being the Sh*t, Y'all Don't Even Know*. Retta also stars as Ruby Hill in NBC's *Good Girls*.

Aziz Ansari (Tom Haverford)

Aziz Ansari has Indian parents, but he has lived his entire life in America. He was born in South Carolina, just like his character Tom. Ansari has performed frequently at the Upright Citizens Brigade Theatre and appeared in the films *I Love You, Man* (2009), *Funny People* (2009) and *Get Him to the Greek* (2010). After the success of *Parks and Recreation*, Ansari went on to create and star in his own series on Netflix, the critically acclaimed *Master of None*, for which he won two Emmys and a Golden Globe for Best Actor – Television Series Musical or Comedy, and was the first Asian–American actor to win a Golden Globe for acting in television.

Jim O'Heir (Jerry Gergich)

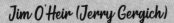

Jim O'Heir first became active in theater and improv during the late 80s and early 90s, training and performing improvisational comedy at Chicago's Second City and as a member of the sketch comedy group White Noise. O'Heir has appeared in several films and made guest appearances on such shows as *Friends, Boston Legal, Malcolm in the Middle, 3rd Rock from the Sun* and *Brooklyn Nine-Nine*. His film credits include *Ed* (1996) and *Seeking a Friend for the End of the World* (2012). After the *Parks and Recreation* series finale, Aubrey Plaza and Jim O'Heir made out on *Late Night with Seth Meyers*, delighting and confusing fans everywhere.

Rob Lowe (Chris Traeger)

Arguably the most famous cast member. Following numerous television roles in the 80s, he became a teen idol and Hollywood star with roles in *The Outsiders* (1983), *Oxford Blues* (1984) and *St. Elmo's Fire* (1985). Lowe is the recipient of two Screen Actors Guild Awards and has been nominated for six Golden Globe awards and a Primetime Emmy Award. Following a 1988 sex tape scandal, Lowe's image suffered, and the job offers slowed down despite his hilarious performance in *Wayne's World* (1992). In the early 2000s he was given a starring role in NBC's political drama *The West Wing*. He starred in a reality show, alongside his sons, called *The Lowe Files*, and in 2018 had his directorial debut with a remake of the 1950s movie *The Bad Seed*.

I don't like getting advice, and I sure as hell don't like being asked to give it. But here we are. Now, take a seat on this chair I made myself when I was five years old. I live my life by some simple rules. I value life, liberty and property. I respect honor, America and, most importantly, breakfast buffets. I like my privacy. I don't trust banks and I don't use them. Sure, I have acquired a significant amount of money during my life. I use it to buy gold, which I bury in a number of secret locations around Pawnee. Actually, scratch that last part. I've said too much.

I hate Europe. I hate anywhere that isn't America. Why would I want to go anywhere else, when everything a man needs is right here in Pawnee? Food and Stuff is where I buy my food. And other stuff. They also sell guns, tools, boots and the steaks that I like. It is equidistant between my home and workplace. I will only attend work functions if bacon-wrapped shrimp is on offer. Or failing that, turkey legs wrapped in bacon. When I go out to eat any meal that isn't breakfast, I go to Mulligan's. I keep a photo album of the steaks I have enjoyed there over the years. Those steaks are like children to me.

A man should keep himself neat, presentable and prepared for anything that might happen – an outbreak of war, terrorism or his ex-wife showing up unexpectedly. Crying is acceptable only at funerals and the Grand Canyon. I have cried twice in my life. Once, when I was seven and I was hit by a school bus. And one other time when I found out that Li'l Sebastian, Pawnee's favorite miniature horse, had passed away.

I strongly believe that there are three acceptable haircuts for a man: high and tight, crew cut, buzz cut. There are two things that every man should have access to at all times – Willie Nelson and a glass of fine scotch. Clear alcohols are for women on diets. Every man should have a dog as a companion. Any dog under 50 pounds is a cat and cats are useless. Every man should have hobbies. I like to work with wood. I also like to collect land mines. I like to read, but only novels about war, tall ships and occasionally meat.

I'll leave you with one last piece of advice. Never half-ass two things. Whole-ass one thing. Now get the hell out of my office.

I KNOW WHAT
I'M ABOUT, SON.

15

Here are some excerpts from my proudest writing achievement – a brief history of everything that has ever happened in Pawnee, entitled *Pawnee: The Greatest Town in America*.

In 1776 a nation was born. Some other unimportant stuff happened after that. Then Pawnee, Indiana was founded in 1817. This event happened to coincide with the driving of the Native American Wamapoke tribe from the land. This is a sensitive issue around Pawnee, especially because City Hall is decorated with several murals that depict the battles with the Wamapoke people. Painted in 1936, one mural depicts the trial of Chief Wamapo, who was accused of the crime of being Indian, was tied to a tree and shot with a cannon. The government of Pawnee worked hard in the following years to ensure that the Wamapoke people were given the respect and rights they deserve. They now preside over the Wamapoke Casino – where the slots are famously "downright filthy."

Another mural depicts the moment in 1817 when the wealthy residents of nearby Eagleton abandoned Pawnee, taking their money with them and leaving the less fortunate citizens behind. But not all of our murals are as confronting. In 1849 Sarah Nelson Quindle exposed her elbow outdoors, which at the time was a Class A felony. Although she felt the law was unjust, she acknowledged that she had broken it and nobly accepted her punishment, which was to be set adrift on a piece of ice on Lake Michigan, like a human popsicle. I kind of like that mural. I see some of myself in her.

Sure, I agree with most people that there are some outdated laws that we should probably get changed. In 1856 the city council banned all sexual positions except for missionary. And two years later they

banned missionary. In 1882 a law was passed that should a Presbyterian speak out of turn, he may be caned across the shin bone. Also, technically any woman caught laughing is deemed a witch. But we definitely don't enforce that. At least I don't think we do.

For a brief time in the 1970s the town was taken over by a cult based on Reasonablism. The cult worships Zorp the Surveyor, a 28-foot-tall lizard with a volcano mouth. According to students of Reasonablism, when Zorp comes to earth, the townspeople's faces will be melted and used as fuel. When the people of Pawnee are forced to engage with Zorp, legend has it that they will take a new form as fleshless chattering skeletons.

One mural at City Hall, which I think is still meaningful today, is that of Lady Justice, an ethereal woman who holds the scales of justice aloft. She is there to remind us we're all equal under the law. A few years ago we repainted the mural to more accurately represent the hulky size of our average citizen.

Leslie Knope

NOW ENTERING PAWNEE
Good Luck With That.

SEASON TWO

The second season kicks off with a South African penguin wedding at the Pawnee Zoo, hosted by Leslie. The ceremony ends with them mating and it is revealed that they are both male. Leslie becomes a local hero to the gay community, including April's two gay boyfriends. Ann and Andy have broken up and Andy has begun living in a tent in the pit behind Ann's house. Meanwhile Ann is hitting it off with Mark, and they start dating with Leslie's blessing, galvanizing the strong friendship and trust between the two women.

Leslie starts dating Dave, a local police officer, after staking out the community garden looking for the person who planted marijuana (it turns out to be carrots). She enlists Ann to help prepare her for their first date, which starts with borrowing an outfit and ends with a booze-fueled practice date culminating in Leslie showing up drunk at Dave's place.

We are introduced to Duke Silver, Ron Swanson's secret musical alter ego, when he is busted by Tom, playing the saxophone on stage in the Duke Silver Trio.

Leslie and Ann take it upon themselves to fill in the pit behind Ann's place without approval, which exposes Andy's hideout when the filling begins. Andy considers suing the Parks Department so that he is financially stable enough to get Ann back, but Leslie convinces him to settle by asking to have the pit permanently filled instead. Andy takes up a job as a shoeshine at City Hall.

Ron and his ex-wife Tammy II are reunited when she offers to help Leslie out with the Library Department's attempt at building a new library on the pit site. Tensions rise between Ron and Tammy, which results in a steamy motel room encounter. Leslie has to step in to break up with Tammy on Ron's behalf, throwing the future of the pit into doubt.

Tom gets divorced, revealing his marriage of convenience with Wendy. Dave asks Leslie to move to San Diego with him, but she declines because she loves Pawnee. We meet Tom's friend and "business partner" Jean-Ralphio. Leslie starts dating Justin (played by Justin Theroux), a handsome, charming friend of Ann's. April and Andy are getting closer, but April is upset by Andy's ongoing obsession with getting Ann back.

By the end of Season 2, we are introduced to Chris and Ben, who are sent to Pawnee to audit the department. Ben is as passionate about accounting as Leslie is about local government. Chris is an appearance-obsessed health freak. Ann breaks up with Mark the week he was going to propose, then gets drunk and kisses Chris. In the midst of a government shutdown, Leslie decides to throw a concert on the pit site. Andy tells April he likes her, but then foolishly kisses Ann in the hospital after crashing his motorcycle.

I love the fourth floor. I heard they sell crystal meth up there, out of a vending machine. There is a guy on the floor who sells jars of urine for people who want to pass drug tests. They had a popcorn machine up there once, but they used the wrong oil, and everyone had to get throat replacements. Ethel Beavers works up there. She is old and gross, and she hates everyone, so I love her.

I hate people but I love Halloween. It's the only time of the year when it's acceptable to cover yourself in fake blood and look at pictures of corpses. All other art sucks and it's gross. My friend Orin does animal performance art. He dresses up like farm animals and you can feed him corn. It's pretty awesome.

When I worked as Ron's assistant it was my job to make sure that nobody bothered him. But making sure people don't bother me is like a full-time job. In the Parks Department, you get a lot of stupid people coming in to complain about lame stuff that I don't care about. The key to avoiding people is not to make eye contact. And if you have to look them in the eye, give them a death stare.

Leslie always wants to talk about her feelings, my feelings and other dumb stuff. I usually just tell her to talk to Ann about it. Ann is a gross nurse and she used to date Andy, so I hate her. Leslie also always wants to hug me. I don't like being touched.

One time I managed to go a whole day without turning on my computer. I hate answering the phone. The phones in this office kind of smell like a butt. I usually just take the phone off the hook, but when I have to answer it I often pretend I can't speak English. Or I just play a Halloween sound effects record from the 1950s into the phone.When I need to escape, I head up to the fourth floor of the building.

1. ONE OF YOUR CO-WORKERS CONFIDES IN YOU THAT THEY ARE GOING TO USE A SICK DAY TO TAKE A LONG WEEKEND AND GO SKIING. WHAT DO YOU DO?

A. What a man does with a sick day is his own damn business. If the government are stupid enough to pay people when they aren't working, then I say go ahead. Take the day and, while you're at it, get the hell out of my office.

B. No, that would never happen in a government department. Those of us who are entrusted to act on behalf of the community would never do such a thing. Wait, what have you heard?

C. Simple. I'd take them into an interrogation room, hold a lamp in their face and demand answers. And if that doesn't work? A karate chop to the jugular.

D. Aw geez, I don't know. Nobody ever asks me this kind of stuff. While you're here can you help me out? I got my belt buckle caught in my chair.

2. HOW DO YOU MOTIVATE THE PEOPLE YOU WORK WITH?

A. Motivate? Good God, woman. If I need someone in the office to do something for me, I just do it myself.

B. I do what anyone would do. I make a plan. Then I make binders. I'll put up a flowchart in the office and rally the team around it while I'm waiting for the motivational team t-shirts to be printed.

C. I just point my weapon at them and ask them to make my day.

D. I stay perfectly still and try not to bother anyone. If I get up and say anything, I usually break something and that can take a lot of their time to clean up.

3. WHICH GOVERNMENT FIGURE INSPIRES YOU THE MOST?

A. I don't respect anyone in government.

B. Jeannette Pickering Rankin. The first woman member of congress.

C. Abraham Lincoln. He is the only president I can think of that shot someone at the movies for blocking his view.

D. Newt Gingrich. He just seems like a really together guy. He's never made a mistake as far as I can recall.

4. WHAT IS THE MOST EFFICIENT WAY TO MANAGE YOUR EMAIL INBOX?

A. I don't use email. That's the first step the internet uses to find out where you live.

B. I respond to every email I get within 40 seconds of receiving it. Doesn't everybody do that?

C. Email? I don't have time for that. Now get me the president on the phone!

D. Email is such a pain in the butt. First you have to find the Alta Vista page, then type in "please go to Yahoo." Then you have to remember your password. I'd prefer it if people just talked to me when they wanted me to do something. But people don't seem to like doing that.

5. HOW SHOULD AN EMPLOYEE DRESS FOR WORK IF THEY WANT A PROMOTION?

A. A man should not dress to be noticed. Clothes are for function only. Smart slacks, a collared shirt and block colors only. Shorts are for women.

B. Pant suits. And those pant suits that have a skirt. Don't wear lime if you are an "autumn" like me.

C. For day work, my FBI jacket and sunglasses. For nighttime work, the same minus the sunglasses plus pajama bottoms.

D. My wife buys all my clothes. I just try not to drop too much food on them when I'm at work.

6. WHAT DOES YOUR WORK AREA LOOK LIKE?

A. I don't own a computer. They are useless. I keep a Claymore land mine on my desk as a message to people who enter my office. I have a bottle of fine scotch in the drawer. They gave me a phone, but I unplugged it.

B. On the wall behind my desk I have framed photos of all the women that inspire me. I keep my desk neat, but in my drawer I keep Sweetums bars and about 40 sugar sachets.

C. When you do the work that I do, the world is your desk. Also, pencils.

D. I do a lot of letter folding, envelope stuffing and stamp licking, so my desk is mostly stacked up with those. They don't let me have sharp objects, which I agree with in theory. But it's hard to eat my lunch when they won't even let me have a spoon.

7. DESCRIBE YOUR PERFECT WORKING DAY

A. That is a trick question. There is no such thing. My perfect day is a Saturday. I'm alone in my workshop, listening to Willie Nelson.

B. I am woken up in Washington by a phone call while staying at Joe and Jill Biden's house. Michelle Obama needs me to help out with her Let's Move! program for kids. So I take my waffles to go and take the Bidens' car out to Michelle's place. After we hash out a plan on her whiteboard, Barack returns from his jog and invites me to stay for dinner and charades.

C. I parasail into a museum to intercept a jewel thief, paralyzing him with a single blow. The president calls me to say that I get to keep the stolen jewels as a reward. Then I make love to Janet Snakehole in the museum gift shop.

D. One time it snowed so much that we didn't have to go in to work – which was lucky because I'd already locked myself out of the house while getting the newspaper in my robe.

8. DESCRIBE YOUR WORST DAY AT WORK?

A. The one day a year when I have to speak to the community and hear their problems. I usually wear headphones, but I can still see their lips move.

B. Probably the time I was so hungover from drinking Tom's Snake Juice that I thought I was dead. Wait, it wasn't such a bad day – my best friend and I took turns barfing into the wastebasket!

C. Working at a shoeshine stand. It smells like Phys Ed.

D. Oh geez, probably the time I split my pants and farted at the same time. No wait, the time I set myself on fire. Actually, I think it was the time I had a heart attack at work.

MOSTLY A

YOU

ARE

Ron

You are a no-nonsense person and most likely a libertarian. When working for the government gets you down, make sure you take time for yourself. This could be as simple as unplugging the phone and locking the door to your office, or as complex as retrieving your ready-made go-bag from its hiding spot and escaping to live inside a mountain forever.

MOSTLY B

YOU ARE

Leslie

It is highly likely that if you are not already running
your workplace, you soon will be. Don't listen to your
co-workers when they say you have too many binders
and put up too many flowcharts around the office.
Keep being the best government employee you can be.
Now sack up, get out there and save the country.
You might be the only one who can!

MOSTLY C

YOU ARE

Burt Macklin

Congratulations because you are awesome. If your boss isn't already paying you a million bucks a year, then you should walk right into their office right now and threaten them with nunchucks. Once they know you are serious, you will probably get promoted and all the ladies will want to date you. Just take it in your stride and always remember to karate chop first and ask questions later!

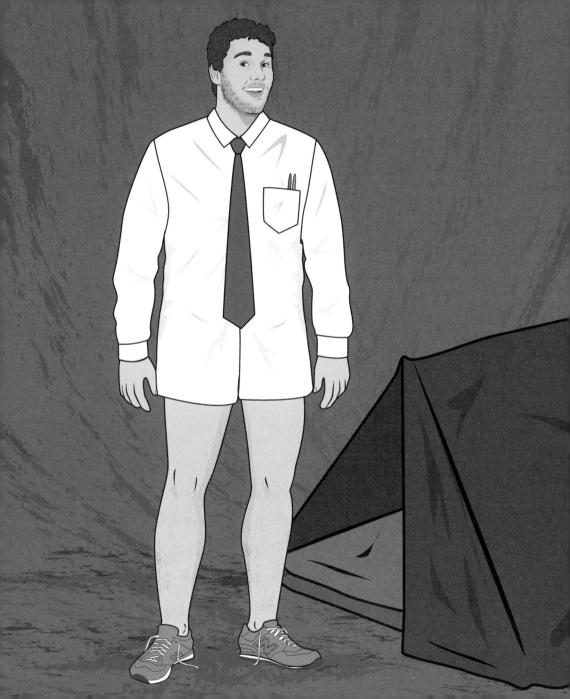

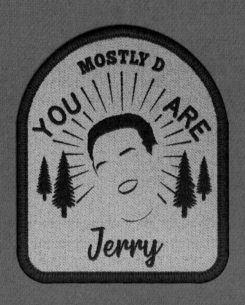

MOSTLY D

YOU ARE

Jerry

Hoo boy. You are the Jerry of the office. It's OK, you just need to stick it out until you retire, maybe in 30 to 50 years from now. Try not to bother your co-workers with your personal life. They are not interested. And try not to set things on fire if you can. Geez, I don't know. Just try to lay low!

SEASON THREE

The government has re-opened after being shut down for three months over the summer and it's Leslie's job to round everyone up from their summer jobs. April has stopped speaking to Andy after he admitted to kissing Ann, and returns from Venezuela with a new boyfriend. Chris tells the team there is no budget and that they are not to take on any new projects. Ben confides in Leslie about his failed mayoral term as a teenager, where he spent the annual budget building a skating rink called Ice Town. Leslie asks Ben and Chris if they can throw a Harvest Festival and use the proceeds to support the department. If they fail, the Parks Department will close down.

Chris and Ann have been dating, but it is time for him to move back to Indianapolis. Ron and Tammy II reunite, when catching up for a coffee to be civil descends into an all-night bender and a shotgun wedding. The Parks team intervene, which fails as Ron and Tammy prepare to head off to their honeymoon in Ron's cabin for a marathon of sex, fueled only by Gatorade and peanuts.

Tom saves the day when he interrupts Tammy's bridal shower in the library and Ron is horrified to see her beating him up. Chris invites April to move to Indianapolis as his assistant but does not invite Ann. Chris breaks up with her but is so sweet about it that she doesn't even realize until the next day.

Ben's Ice Town controversy comes back to bite him when the media find out in the lead-up to the Harvest Festival. Leslie defends him to a local reporter, and it slips out that she thinks he is attractive. Ben's catastrophic appearance on *Ya' Heard with Perd* throws the Harvest Festival sponsorship into jeopardy. April and Andy make up after he does all of her "work" for the day, including giving Donna and Jerry a foot rub.

Leslie arranges miniature horse Li'l Sebastian for the Harvest Festival, who is a phenomenon in the town. He goes missing but is eventually found in the corn maze. The Harvest Festival is a success despite this controversy. Andy and April move in together and throw a dinner party, which turns out to be a surprise wedding after just a month of dating. Chris has a rule that co-workers can't date, but Leslie and Ben are getting closer. The rivalry with Eagleton is reignited when Eagleton puts a fence around their park to keep Pawnee kids out.

Chris sends Ben and Leslie on a business trip to win a bid to host a baseball game, with no idea of the sexual tension between them. Leslie tries to temper things with a mix CD of whale sounds, Mandarin lessons and banjo music, but it's not enough. Ben is making all the right moves and makes an inspiring speech about Pawnee, winning the bid. Ben and Leslie go out for dinner at a romantic restaurant and Ben admits his feelings.

Leslie is about to give in when Chris shows up to congratulate them. He invites them to stay at his condo in the town. Leslie and Ben are finally left alone. They kiss.

The season ends with Ann starting her part-time job in PR at Parks. Ben and Leslie are hiding their relationship. Li'l Sebastian dies, and the Parks Department throws a memorial with the help of Tom and Jean-Ralphio's new business, Entertainment 720. Leslie is approached to become a candidate for mayor. Leslie says yes, throwing her relationship with Ben into further doubt.

Today we are gathered to celebrate the life of Indiana's favorite miniature horse, Li'l Sebastian – our hero, our mascot and our reason to get out of bed in the morning. At this memorial service, we will celebrate the life of Li'l Sebastian as it should be. Especially after our minute's silence was so callously interrupted by the office cleaner walking past listening to "Man! I Feel Like a Woman" by Shania Twain.

Li'l Sebastian, we already miss you and we know that the hardest days without you are still to come. But it fills us with hope to know that you are now in heaven, looking down on us while you do your two favorite things: eating carrots and urinating freely. In lieu of flowers, we ask that on your way out, you make a donation to Li'l Sebastian's favorite charity, The Afghan Institute of Learning.

To everyone's favorite Pawneean, I raise this glass of carrot juice. Li'l Sebastian – your body may be buried in the lot behind the mall, but your spirit will never leave our hearts and our memories. Like many of us gathered here today, Li'l Sebastian loved the simple things in life. A full trough of water, a bucket overflowing with oats and a willing sexual partner. In fact two of his former lovers, Coconut and Lady Bug, are here today. Oh boy, Coconut is pooping on the stage. Can someone get a mop and bucket?

THE BEST OF
The Duke Silver Trio

From the hit albums *Smooth as Silver*, *Hi Ho Duke* and *Memories of Now*, comes the definitive *Best of The Duke Silver Trio*, out now on record and compact disc where all good jazz is sold.

Why Don't You Blow on
My Sax Tonight?

I've Got an Itch That Only
Jazz Can Scratch

A Man's Word Is Sacred

Rest in Jazz

Slide into a Warm Tub Full
of My Jazz

It Might Be Cold Outside,
But It's About to Get Warm
All Up in My Jazz

Someone Please Tell Me
What's Wrong with My Jazz

Sax Hurts in the Morning

A Half Empty Glass of Jazz

Someone Got Jazz in My Eyes

"I found a sandwich in one of your parks and I want to know why it didn't have mayonnaise?"

"There's a sign at Ramsett Park that says 'Do not drink the sprinkler water,' so I made Sun Tea with it and now I have an infection."

"I found a raccoon in my car eating all the garbage I left on my back seat when I went hiking at Pawnee Lake. How was I supposed to know you shouldn't leave your windows open?"

"I bought a house near the Sweetums factory and all of my husband's hair fell out. Now I don't want to have sex with him anymore."

COMPLAINTS FROM
Pawnee Locals

"My dog went to one of your parks and ate another dog's feces and I am going to sue you for that."

"I've been eating lasagne and muffins every day of my life for 40 years and I feel terrible."

"I left my Christmas tree on the curb for seven weeks and nobody removed it."

"I got sent a coupon book for Paunch Burger and ate their food every day for a month. Now I can't poop. What are you going to do about it?"

TOM'S

Failed Business Ideas

AT THE RISK OF BRAGGING, ONE OF THE THINGS I'M BEST AT IS RIDING COATTAILS. BEHIND EVERY SUCCESSFUL MAN IS ME. SMILING AND TAKING PARTIAL CREDIT.

I might work for the Parks Department but as far as this playa is concerned, my full-time job is being Pawnee's sexiest and swaggiest young entrepreneur. I've dabbled in lots of businesses, like when Jean-Ralphio and I started the global multimedia business Entertainment 720. Why did we call it that? Because we were willing to go around the world twice for our clients. Now I don't know why that business failed, but we were bankrupt before we even got our first client!

Let me take you through some of my best ideas. I invented a unisex perfume called Tommy Fresh, but the perfume company I pitched it to hated it. I even had a toddler cologne called Baby, You Smell Good. I invented Saltweens – Saltines for tweens. Snail Mail – that's home-delivery escargot. I made my own hand-clapping dimmer switch for my house. Whenever I've got a boo on my couch, I just clap my hands. The lights dim and my stereo plays some sweet Boyz II Men.

Y'all ever tried Snake Juice? That was my revolutionary high-end Kahlua-style liqueur. Everyone loved it at the launch party, but a couple of people had to go to the hospital afterward to get their tummies pumped. So it's off the market now. And don't forget the Talking Tissue Box that says "Blow that nose, playa" or "Someone's got the sniffies" whenever you take a tissue out!

The closest I've ever been to success was Rent-A-Swag. I was inspired to start renting out my designer clothes to teenagers when I realized that I was roughly the same size as the average Pawnee 12-year-old. Also I totally invented LASIK for fingernails – a laser that cuts your fingernails (you'll never have to cut them again!) ... but someone else must have come up with it at the same time, because everybody is doing it in Beverly Hills now.

I guess not every business I've had has failed. I went into real estate with Donna once to sell Ron's cabin and split that commish! Wait, that kind of failed too. I've still got business dreams for the future. Like taking the wheels off private jets and turning them into houses, so people can live in their own private jet! One day I plan to make a remake of *Point Break* where I play both roles, Keanu and Swayze.

Oh, and I've got high hopes for DJ Roomba 2!

JERRY'S SECRETS TO A

Happy Marriage

People at the office don't seem very interested in my personal life. In fact they usually leave the room when I start talking about myself. And come to think of it, they leave when I talk about work too. Please, pull up a chair and I'll tell you my secrets to a happy marriage. No, not that chair. I got cracker crumbs all over that one.

Gayle is the only woman I have ever been with and I wouldn't have it any other way. Some people said we were too young to get married, but I was 24 years old and just wanted to start our life together. When Gayle took my virginity on our wedding night, I felt like the luckiest guy on earth. We like to keep a routine in our family. Breakfast together, singing together, baths together. Gayle just loves to get me in the tub and give me a good scrub. I get all kinds of stuff stuck to me during the day.

I think you should always talk about your marital problems when they come up and never go to bed angry at each other. I remember when I came home and told Gayle I'd lost my wedding ring for the fourth time. Boy oh boy was she mad. She turns into a real grumpy goose and will say things like "Hey Mr. Forgetful" or the "B" word – Bozo. Those words rattle around my head for hours.

We love to take a holiday together every year. I know Muncie's not glamorous – people call it America's number one flyover city, but we like it. There's never any lines at the airport and all the restaurants are empty most of the time.

Can I please go now? Gayle is making a roast and I locked my keys in the car.

A DAY IN THE LIFE OF

Jean-Ralphio
and Mona-Lisa

JEAN-RALPHIO: Yo, come over here pretty. Turn that frown upside dizzity! This party is off the CHURT. Let me introduce you to the second-best looking person in town, my twin sister from the same mister, Mona-Lisa. She's so cray cray. She once jumped out of a moving car to buy a Nicki Minaj poster.

MONA-LISA: No I didn't! Next you're gonna tell her I sells fake ecstasy to kids.

JEAN-RALPHIO: But you really do that.

MONA-LISA: And I really did jump outta that car. PSYCH! Me and Jean-Ralphio do everything together. Including asking our dad for money. MONEY PWEASE!

JEAN-RALPHIO: At least I didn't sleep with our cousin.

JEAN-RALPHIO: We sometimes get asked to do threesomes together but it's not weird.

MONA-LISA: But we do get Brazilians together and that can be weird.

MONA-LISA: I frenched my cousin one time. I might still be in love with him. Or pregnant to him. PSYCH! I'm not pregnant. I always practice safe sex and I don't want to spread diseases.

JEAN-RALPHIO: That's why I love my sister, she's so thoughtful. Just kidding! She's the WOOORST person in the world. Whenever my friends want to date her, I'm like drop the microphone, get outta that bitch!

MONA-LISA: Shut up! And gimme some money, Mona-Lisa needs a drinky-wink.

JEAN-RALPHIO: She always hits me up for money now. I got run over by a Lexus and got a payout. I always find a way to make ends meet, even though I've never worked a day in my life. When life gives ya lemons, you sell some of your grandma's jewelry and you go clubbin'.

MONA-LISA: DAYAYUM. I'm outta here. I think I see Jared Leto over there.

ANDY'S GUIDE TO
Getting Your Girl Back

When Ann dumped me, I did what any normal guy would do if that happened to them. I started living in the vacant pit next to her house in a tent so I could keep an eye on her. I still don't really understand why she left. The last three months was the best time of my life. I got to sit on the couch all day while she brought me snacks and beer and cleaned up after me. I just don't get why she didn't think that was awesome like I did.

I tried super hard to get Ann back after she dumped me, even when she started dating Mark. Mark is an idiot. I tried to prove my love for her by beating Mark at pool. The prize? Ann's love. I beat Mark fair and square. But for some dumb reason she still didn't want to be my girlfriend, even after watching me kick his ass. One time Mark was over at Ann's place for a date. I was watching from the pit, but it started to rain pretty hard, so Mark let me come in and eat with them. I don't care, I still think that Mark sucks.

Women love surprises. When I was trying to get April to date me, I knew one thing. Women are queens. And queens deserve flowers and massages, chocolate, booze, diamonds, rubies, emeralds, those treasure chests full of scarves, different kinds of lubes that warm up when you rub them on stuff. Women also like jewelry. When I proposed to April I bought her a ring pop, but then I ate it before I got around to asking her.

If you want to get the woman of your dreams, you have to make them know they are special. I made a cool shrine to Ann around my shoeshine station. I put up a bunch of cute photos of her, including one of her in a bikini. For some reason she didn't really like that. Whenever I think my woman is mad at me, I make a list of all the things I have done and then try not to do them anymore.

And if that doesn't work? Turn up naked. Women love that!

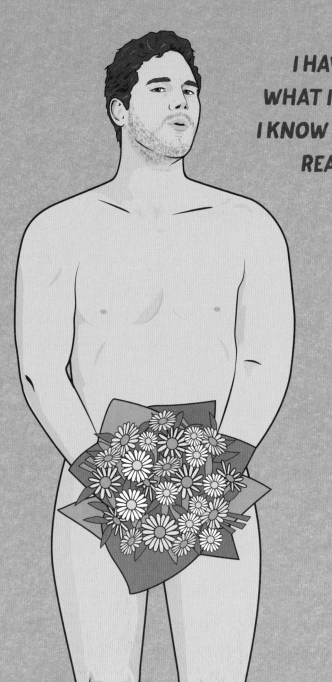

I HAVE *NO IDEA*
WHAT I'M DOING BUT
I KNOW I DO IT REALLY,
REALLY WELL.

47

SEASON FOUR

At the conclusion of the Li'l Sebastian memorial, we find that Leslie has accepted the offer to run for public office, which means she has to break up with Ben to avoid a scandal. Ron has fled to his cabin after his first wife, Tammy I, returned to Pawnee. Amidst the scandal of a government staffer sending a photo of his penis to all the women in the department, Leslie tries to avoid being alone with Ben to delay their inevitable breakup. Leslie flees to Ron's cabin, and they make a pact to face their problems head on. When Leslie tries to break up with Ben, he presents her with a gift – a "Knope 2012" pin, sealing their fate. Leslie's place of birth becomes controversial when it turns out she was born in Eagleton, Pawnee's rival town. Tom and Jean-Ralphio's Entertainment 720 is in full swing, despite lacking a business model and client. They hire professional basketballers and beautiful women on outrageous salaries. Tom takes over Leslie's function for local businesses by branding the entire event with photos and rugs with his face on them. Tom reveals at the party that Entertainment 720 is already bankrupt. They throw one final bankruptcy party and Tom's love interest Lucy shows up. They kiss. Ron offers Tom his old job back.

Chris starts dating Jerry's daughter, Millicent, which Jerry initially approves of, but Chris's honesty about what they are getting up to and public displays of affection freak Jerry out. Millicent stops returning Chris's calls after four dates, so he enlists Ann's help to work out why he scares women off.

Ben and Leslie try to stay friends, but tempers flare at the model UN conference. Ben decides to step back from the Parks Department and focus on other matters.

Leslie confronts Ben and tells him she wants to be with him. They decide to get back together, despite the risk of scandal. They tell Chris and he launches an investigation and ethics trial of Knope, resulting in her being suspended for two weeks with pay. After the scandal, Leslie's poll support drops to 1 percent and her campaign advisors quit. The parks team takes over managing the campaign. She will be running against Bobby Newport, heir to the Sweetums candy fortune.

If Bobby Newport wins, Chris could lose his job for helping Leslie with her campaign. Leslie debates Bobby on TV. A porn star, Brandi Maxxxx, aligns herself with Leslie. Bobby threatens that Sweetums will move to Mexico if Leslie wins. Leslie's final speech steals the show, with a promise to put Pawnee first. Bobby's father Nick Newport dies and Leslie makes a series of public gaffes, including driving her campaign bus through his memorial service.

The season ends with Bobby Newport's campaign manager Jen offering Ben a job to run a congressional campaign in Washington for six months. Leslie doesn't want Ben to leave, but she encourages Ben to go to Washington. Bobby Newport wins the election. All Leslie can do is laugh "Because my dream is dead." After demanding a recount, it turns out that Leslie has won by 21 votes, and the team celebrate.

I know everyone thinks that accounting is boring, but it's not. I don't want to brag about it, but they call me the Swiss army accountant. Well, they don't really. But they should. I will happily stay up all night if I have to, just to ensure that a company has amortized all of its intangible assets at the correct rate. But I haven't always been good with money. When I was mayor of Partridge at age 18, I blew the whole year's budget on an ice skating rink called Ice Town. It failed and I was ostracized by the community. Some people say I never recovered from this, but that's simply not true. I only scream out in my sleep once or twice a week these days, according to Leslie. Three times max now that *Game of Thrones* is over.

The best thing about accounting is the jokes. Accountants have the best jokes! You can ac-count on us to make you laugh. Unless you are a lawyer. They have their own jokes and don't seem to get ours. One time I was out in Baltimore doing an audit and I told their lawyer that their accruals had been entered incorrectly, resulting in a loss of $140,000 for the fiscal year. He started crying, and then I said to him, "Sorry to make such a-cruel joke." Probably one of the finest puns of my career. He didn't really laugh. I guess you had to be there.

I try to use my knowledge to help the people that I love, but it's not always easy. Leslie spends a lot of our money on gifts for Ann. Last year she spent over $4,000 on poster and banner printing. When I lived with April and Andy I had to stop Andy from putting house bills directly into the freezer. Oh, yeah. That's about as useful as leveraging QuickBooks Pro to audit the federal government's foreign exchange losses!

If I wasn't an accountant I'd love to have my own calzone restaurant. I developed a complex formula for the perfect dough-to-filling ratio for my homemade calzones. I call it my formula "for mula!" My dream is to own a restaurant called The Low Cal Calzone Zone. Man, I just don't understand why everyone likes pizza so much.

Anyway, I have to go now. I have an interview for a very exciting job opportunity – to do internal accounting for an accounting firm! Calc-u-later!

LIVING A ZEN LIFE

with Chris Traeger

There is *literally* nothing more important to me than living a healthy, balanced life. Some people think that working out a few times a week, downloading a mindfulness app or cutting out red meat is enough. That is simply incorrect. I dedicate all 24 hours of my day to achieving a state of ultimate fitness and Zen. If there was a 25th hour in the day, I can assure you I would make use of that too. I was born with a rare blood disorder and my parents were told I only had three weeks to live. I am now 44 years old and no doctor can tell me how this happened. I'm featured in several medical textbooks.

When I wake up at 5 am, the first thing I do is stretch, while staring at my naked body in a full-length mirror. After 20 minutes of "self-reflection stretching," it's time for an egg white, chia seed and beet smoothie before my pre-dawn jog. I always try to race the sun, although after my smoothie I often have to "beet" my way through the dark to the bathroom. Once I completed my fitness goal of the four-minute mile, I took it up a notch. My new goal is to run to the moon.

I need to maintain my body fat at a constant 2.8 percent. My perfect meal is anything with balanced macronutrients. I consume nothing that is fried, and I avoid all meat. That is unless Ron is threatening me with a sharp object, which happens more often than I'd like. Looking at my body, you might think that I have an exercise regime that is extreme. I simply don't agree. It may surprise you to hear that I am not a member of any health clubs in Pawnee. The world is my gym. When I have a meeting on a different floor, I always take the stairs. And I walk backwards to get there. On one leg. This is why I have the same resting heart rate as a 100-year-old tortoise.

I keep myself very hydrated and urinate roughly 12 times a night. And those nighttime steps add up. My healthy urethra tip: Eat plenty of radishes. I also meditate and do yoga every day, but recently I have been partaking in daily psychotherapy sessions with Dr. Nygard, which really seem to be helping. I didn't think it was possible to cry that much in one hour. That's why I always bring two liters of coconut water and an absorbent towel to each session to rehydrate.

My dermatologist told me that I have the skin of an 18-year-old woman who has never seen the sun. But I have the same skin routine as the average man, and I keep it simple. After cleansing, I open up my pores with a face steamer infused with peppermint oils. I apply a mask made from bentonite clay that is hand-picked from the ground for me by a delightful team of people in Wyoming. Then I moisturize with a cream I have specially formulated in Japan that contains local seaweed and beta-carotene. I like to keep my own stash of beta-carotene just to top up on the side. I once took too much and my left lung collapsed. But the surgeon said I looked 30 years younger so all up it was a great day for me.

I imagine this might all sound like a lot to your average person. But I don't want to be average. I plan to live until I am 150. I really don't want to die. I can't ever die.

THE WORLD IS MY GYMNASIUM.

I'M PERD HAPLEY AND

These Are My Thoughts

Hi, I'm TV's Perd Hapley and these are my thoughts. It's the show where I, Perderick L. Hapley describe my thoughts to the viewers. That's you. Let's begin this segment by starting it. Right at the conclusion of this sentence.

On today's episode of *These Are My Thoughts*, I will start off by introducing the show. Right after that I will describe the stories that are going to be on the show. Like I will do right now.

Issue number one is the first issue we're going to talk about. On tonight's show, our first topic is "Obamacare," which I understand is short for "Alabamacare." Directly after that story, we will take a commercial break, where you, the viewer will have the option to watch commercials.

After the commercial break, we will be joined by a person, Leslie Knope. Also joining us today is a different person. Leslie Knope will sit on that couch over there, and I will ask her questions, which she will answer. I will know what questions to ask, because they are written on cue cards for me. I did not write the questions, but I am allowed to ask them to people who sit on my couch.

Sometimes there is a segment called "Film Thoughts," where I watch a film and then tell you what I thought of it. *E.T.* is a film I have watched. It's a heartwarming story but it's just not believable, which is why I gave it one and a half stars.

OK, my producer is making his finger do a circle, like he is winding something up. In this industry, we call that a wind-up.

I'm Perd Hapley, and this is the end of my thoughts. And I just realized I am not holding my microphone.

SEASON FIVE

Leslie and Andy are visiting Ben and April in Washington while applying for a federal grant to clean up the Pawnee River. Leslie is overwhelmed by the scale of what goes on there compared to Pawnee and Ben's exposure to important people, including "tall attractive women" in Washington. In reality, Ben is also struggling, finding himself unpopular with the interns. Leslie has started her job as a councilwoman and her first act is to propose a tax on sugar, which proves unpopular with the community. Andy is trying to get into the police academy but is struggling with the physical training. Ron meets single mom Diane when he takes it upon himself to fix a pothole in front of her house. He takes her daughters trick or treating but struggles to know what to do with them.

Leslie leases a house to surprise Ben on his scheduled return to Pawnee. However, Ben has been offered a job to run a congressional campaign in Florida. He returns to Pawnee and proposes to Leslie in their new home, deciding to stay. Leslie tries to bring Ben's parents back to civil terms by sewing them a unity quilt, but leaves off Ben's dad's much younger girlfriend, causing more problems.

Ron gives Tom money for his startup idea, Rent-A-Swag, where he rents out his designer clothes to middle school children. Ron wins an award for his woodcrafting of a chair and Tammy II shows up to try and tempt him away. He evades her and takes Diane to see him perform as Duke Silver. During Leslie's bachelorette party at Ann's house, they find the pit site being filled in to build a Paunch Burger. Leslie decides on a drunken whim to bury a bunch of Wamapoke Indian artefacts in there so that they can't build on it. The ladies spend the rest of the night digging them up, while the boys have a fantastic night.

Ann decides she wants to have a baby and starts searching for a sperm donor. Andy gets 100 percent on his written police exam but fails the personality test. Ben and Leslie throw a gala to raise money for the park construction and they reach their goal of $50,000. They decide not to wait three months and to get married that night, mobilizing the Parks team to organize the logistics. Late on a snowy Pawnee evening, Ron walks Leslie down the aisle, but the ceremony is almost ruined by disgruntled councilman Jeremy Jamm, who Ron punches, resulting in him being locked up. Leslie and Ben get married in the Parks office, surrounded by their friends.

Ben takes a job at Sweetums, running their charity division. Ann asks Chris to be her sperm donor, and he says yes. Jerry is retiring and Ann and Ben take him on a bucket list day. Leslie joins Jerry and his family for breakfast and decides she wants to start a family with Ben. Ann and Chris chicken out at the fertility clinic before the sperm donation, go home and decide to conceive the old fashioned way. Andy finds a positive pregnancy test in Ron's cabin after a brainstorming weekend away and his alter ego Burt Macklin is on the case. Tom is made an offer to buy Rent-A-Swag. He says no and the mystery buyer then decides to set up a rival business across the road. April gets into veterinary school. The season ends with the revelation that Diane is pregnant with Ron's baby.

RON SWANSON'S LOVE INTERESTS

Before I discuss my personal business, let me get one thing straight. The perfect woman is Steffi Graf. She is tall, has a strong back and is versatile across all playing surfaces. After I make love to a woman, I like to wear a red shirt and black pants. Sometimes I bring in breakfast for the whole office.

My first wife, Tammy I, works for the IRS and has the tracking ability and the body odor of a bloodhound. She was present at my birth and assisted in the delivery as she was at that time a candy striper at the hospital. I don't like to admit it to everyone, but she turns me into a wimp when she is around. She once held a blade to my throat and said to me "I was there the minute you were born, and I intend to be there the minute you die."

My second wife was also named Tammy, but I don't believe in coincidences or tradition for that matter. My mother's name is Tamara but I don't think that really means anything. Tammy II once put a push pin in my head when I broke up with her. I truly believe that she cannot be killed. That woman turns me into a sex maniac. Our lovemaking is so intense that sometimes I don't know where my flesh stops and hers begins. She occasionally drops back into my life to remind me she is immortal. When she is nearby, I can smell the burning sulfur coming off her hooves. She tries to mask it with her favorite perfume, Girth, but I can smell her regardless.

If I found out the world was going to end tomorrow. I'd go home and drink some whiskey. Then I'd go see my ex-wives so I could watch them meet their fiery end with my own eyes.

I once dated Wendy, Tom's ex-wife. I liked her, but then she asked me to move to Canada to be with her. Canada! I don't need to tell you what my answer was.

When I met Diane I realized that I'd finally met my match. She doesn't take any crap and knows how to unblock a sink. She has kids and that means I've had to change some aspects of my life. Like eating ethnic food sometimes. But only if it has the word "meat" in the name.

THE KEY TO BURNING AN EX-WIFE EFFIGY IS TO DIP IT IN PARAFFIN WAX AND THEN TOSS THE FLAMING BOTTLE OF ISOPROPYL ALCOHOL FROM A SAFE DISTANCE. DO NOT STAND TOO CLOSE WHEN YOU LIGHT AN EX-WIFE EFFIGY.

THE BEAUTY OF Breakfast Foods

When they shut down Mulligan's Steakhouse, I changed my focus to breakfast foods only. When I'm not at JJ's Diner enjoying my favorite breakfast – all the eggs and bacon they have on the premises – I like to prepare my breakfast at home.

I don't understand why anyone eats anything else but breakfast foods.

Let's start with the basics. Every man's fridge should include the following items: at least four pounds of bacon, two dozen eggs and as much red meat as you can fit in the remaining space.

You forgot the waffles. I usually get mine from JJ's Diner, but if you have to eat breakfast at home, you're going to need to have a couple gallons of waffle batter in the fridge at all times. And don't forget whipped cream. Don't skimp on quality either – like most things, the best version comes out of an aerosol can.

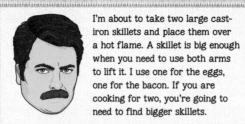

I'm about to take two large cast-iron skillets and place them over a hot flame. A skillet is big enough when you need to use both arms to lift it. I use one for the eggs, one for the bacon. If you are cooking for two, you're going to need to find bigger skillets.

Ron, do you have any coffee in this place? I like mine with extra cream. And 30 sugars.

I only drink coffee when I am at work, to numb the pain. Once the bacon is crispy enough to open an envelope with, I plate it up with the eggs. Then I take a fork, sit down in my chair and shut the hell up. Don't get me wrong. I don't just eat bacon and eggs for breakfast. When the weather is right, I've been known to cook up a batch of bacon-wrapped breakfast shrimp. Oh, and my favorite non-breakfast meal is called turf and turf. It's a 16 ounce t-bone and a 24 ounce porterhouse. I enjoy this with a whiskey and a cigar, which I consume all at the same time because I'm a free American.

SE

That sounds delicious. Does it come with any sides?

Do not, and I cannot stress this more strongly, add vegetables.

NEW!
Triple Paunch Burger

Only in the densely corn-encrusted state of Indiana, where we have access to so much surplus high-fructose corn syrup, could we have the ability to adequately fatten the portly hogs and cattle that go into making every Paunch Burger. We hand-select every animal that goes into our burgers and ensure that they are well cared for, from their first days in the Pawnee Industrial Stock Birthing Facility to their final moments on the killing floor.

Come on in and try our new Triple Paunch Burger. It comes with all four kinds of meat: beef, pork, chicken and tacos. Why not pair it with bacon-wrapped onion rings for only $6.99. Or you can add a fried egg for just 50 cents!

Feeling thirsty? Try our 512 ounce "child size" soda for $1.59. It's the size of a two-year-old child, in liquid form!

Watching your weight? We've got you covered with Water Zero: It tastes just like water, but sweeter (the "zero" refers to the amount of water in the drink). And it's only 300 calories. We are also proud to introduce our new healthy choice beverage, Diet Water Zero Lite, coming in at only 60 calories.

Healthy food is for suckers. It tastes like garbage and if you say you like it, you're a chump and a liar!

Sure, we might have some rivals in Pawnee, like Colonel Plump's Slop Trough (formerly Sue's Salads). But as soon as you enter one of our 15 Pawnee locations and the smell hits you, you'll soon see why we are the number one fast-food chain in southern Indiana.

Put it in your body or you're a nerd!

A Message From the CEO of Sweetums

Here at Sweetums we have a mission to be America's favorite candy company. As Pawnee's number one supplier of candy and local jobs, we will not rest until every man, woman, child and pet has a Sweetums product inside them. In order to reach this goal, we are proud to announce that this year we will be sponsoring the Indiana School Lunch Program. Every school-aged child will have access to our five top-selling candies and sodas in their daily cafeteria meal. We are also moving into catering for Indiana retirement homes, in a joint venture with a pharmaceutical company that is Indiana's number one supplier of insulin and cannot be named in this message for legal reasons.

On a sad note, we are keen to move forward as a company after the Sweetums molasses plant explosion earlier this year. Due to no fault of our own, there was a catastrophic failure in one of our sugar cane boilers while it was left unattended over lunch, resulting in one of the slowest ecological disasters that Indiana has ever seen. Tragically, a lot of homes in Pawnee were very gradually flooded with delicious Sweetums molasses. Sadly some lives were lost when several of the larger Pawneeans were unable to maneuver themselves out of their sweetness-filled homes.

You also may have heard some media reports of late stating that there are rat parts in the chocolate that goes into Sweetums candy. We can say categorically that these reports are inaccurate. At Sweetums we are passionate about minimizing waste and conserving our natural resources. This is why we insist on using the entire carcass in all our animal-based candies. We truly care about the health of our customers. That's why we also work closely with the Surgeon General to ensure that their warning labels are clearly placed on all of our products.

Finally, Sweetums would like to thank the city of Pawnee for their loyalty to our products, and for contributing to making Indiana the biggest, heaviest consumers of high-fructose corn syrup-based candies in the country. Remember, "If ya can't beat 'em, Sweetums."

SEASON SIX

Season 6 opens with Ron proposing to Diane, deciding on a whim to get married on the fourth floor with Leslie and April present. Ann is pregnant. The mystery buyer of Rent-A-Swag is revealed to be Jean-Ralphio and Mona-Lisa's father, Dr. Saperstein, in an act of misguided revenge for all of his kids' problems that they have blamed on Tom. Andy and Ben go to London to meet Lord Edgar Covington, a potential benefactor for their after-school music program charity. Covington hits it off with Andy and invites him to stay and work with him. April's veterinary school orientation does not go well, and she quits.

Eagleton is bankrupt after massive expenditure, including filling the public pool with bottled water. After initially rubbing it in, Leslie hatches a plan to help them and win the recall election. Eagleton will be dissolved and reabsorbed into Pawnee, to be celebrated by a Unity Concert. We meet Craig Middlebrooks, the neurotic Eagleton animal control manager who joins the team. Leslie gets voted out of office, then spirals into a depression. Ben and Leslie drown their sorrows and Ann saves them at the last moment before they get tattoos at the local pawn shop. Ann convinces Leslie to give her last month in office all of her energy. Tom sells Rent-A-Swag.

Leslie goes up against Sweetums when she wants to put fluoride in the water supply, but they want to add sugar. This results in Ben getting fired from his job at Sweetums. This lasts a week before Ben accepts the job he has taken and quit twice, at the local accounting firm. Leslie's last day has her deciding to run for a seat on city council, but the team tries to convince her it's a bad idea. Jennifer Barkley convinces Leslie she has a future doing bigger things. Ben takes Leslie to Paris. On her return she comes back to the job of Deputy Director of the Parks Department. Chris proposes to Ann and she says yes.

Andy performs at a birthday party and discovers his skills as a children's entertainer, Johnny Karate. Ann and Chris say farewell to Pawnee. Leslie throws a huge party covering all the holidays they will miss spending together. Ron's son John is born. Leslie is offered a job running a branch of the National Parks Service in Chicago. Ben suggests that Tom uses his money to start a dry cleaning holding company, but Tom pitches an idea for an Italian restaurant, Tom's Bistro, to an investor at the last moment. Ann has her baby and Leslie rushes to her side.

In the lead-up to the Unity Concert. Leslie finds out she is pregnant and calls Ben while he is drunk on blueberry wine at a local winery with Ron, but the call is cut off. When he returns, he tells Leslie he realizes he wants to start a family and Leslie tells him her happy news. Ben and Leslie are shocked to find out they are having triplets. Donna reconnects with her ex, Joe. Leslie announces to the team that she has taken the job in Chicago. The Unity Concert is a success, with Andy leading an all-star singalong of "Bye Bye Li'l Sebastian" with Ron as Duke Silver on the sax. After a disastrous soft open, the official opening night of Tom's Bistro is a success. Everyone turns down Leslie's job offers to work with her in Chicago, so Leslie negotiates to do her new job from Pawnee.

We skip ahead to three years later, where we see Leslie running the Midwest division of the National Parks Service, with the whole team and her triplets by her side.

For some reason people always think I am upset BUT I'M NOT! There's nothing wrong with a grown man raising his voice sometimes. When I wanted a job at Tom's restaurant he told me I had to "take it down a notch." A NOTCH?! I'LL TAKE IT DOWN A THOUSAND NOTCHES IF I HAVE TO!

I used to run the dog shelter in Eagleton until we were merged into Pawnee. Of course I was sad, because I just wanted to run that shelter on my own. Why can't it be about Craig JUST ONE DAMN TIME? I thought, first my cousin Winona gets into a car accident the night my one-man show opens and now THIS? WHY ARE MY ACCOMPLISHMENTS ALWAYS OVERSHADOWED?!!

My last boyfriend said I was crazy. He said I should see a doctor about my anger problems! Oh, I have a medical condition all right – it's called caring too much. AND IT'S INCURABLE. Also I have eczema.

Everyone in the Parks Department seems to be coupling off these days. Oh it's so cute I WANT TO THROW UP AND KILL MYSELF! If I don't meet someone soon I swear I WILL BURN THIS PLACE TO THE GROUND!

That's it, I AM GOING TO LOSE IT. Somebody follow me! I AM DISTRAUGHT.

I've had enough of this. I NEED TO GO LIE DOWN FOR 45 MINUTES. NO, AN HOUR!

Billy Eichner as Craig Middlebrooks

Craig Middlebrooks enters our lives screaming in Season 6, when he moves over from the Eagleton animal control department and hits it off with his Pawnee equivalent, Donna. Middlebrooks is seemingly unable to express himself at a regular volume and is prone to overreacting. We love Craig because he represents the rage trapped inside all of us. He just can't help but let it out.

Billy Eichner is the star, executive producer and creator of *Billy on the Street with Billy Eichner*, a comedy game show where he asks members of the public questions while walking through a city, often accompanied by a celebrity. For this role, Eichner was nominated for a Daytime Emmy Award for Outstanding Game Show Host in 2013. In 2019 Eichner provided the voice of Timon in Disney's live action remake of *The Lion King*.

Alison Becker as Shauna Malwae-Tweep

Shauna Malwae-Tweep, the intrepid and beautiful *Pawnee Journal* reporter, makes occasional appearances on the show. She is always first on the scene for a government story and frequently becomes romantically involved with male characters, usually in the form of a one-night stand. Leslie is crushed when Shauna sleeps with Mark after being interviewed about the Lot 48 pit. This is closely followed by Shauna being crushed when Mark shuts down any ideas of a future romance between them.

Much like the rest of the cast, Alison Becker has improv experience and is still a regular player at the Upright Citizens Brigade Theatre in New York City. She was previously the host of VH1's *Top 20 Video Countdown* and has appeared in commercials for Dairy Queen and Chrysler.

Paul Schneider as Mark Brendanawicz

Although he was only in the show for Seasons 1 and 2, Mark Brendanawicz certainly made his mark romantically. Initially the object of Leslie's affections after a one-night stand three years before Season 1 began, Mark is very taken by Ann Perkins and, when they begin to date, he spends most of his time fending off Ann's ex, Andy, who is trying everything to get her back.

In 2014, Schneider said of his time on *Parks and Recreation*: "That experience was very strange for me. You know, I signed up for a specific character that was changed in mid-season ... And, all of a sudden, I was kind of confused and kind of having a lot less to do."

Schneider is best known for his portrayal of Dick Liddil in *The Assassination of Jesse James by the Coward Robert Ford* (2007). He has also starred in the films *All the Real Girls* (2003), *Elizabethtown* (2005) and *Lars and the Real Girl* (2007). Schneider won a National Society of Film Critics Award for Best Supporting Actor in *Bright Star* (2009).

Bill Murray as Mayor Gunderson

Comedic superstar Bill Murray made his mark on *Parks and Recreation* when he appeared as Mayor Gunderson, as a corpse and in videos that made up part of his memorial service. During the funeral, it is revealed that Gunderson was sleeping with elderly fourth-floor stenographer Ethel Beavers. She claims that "for 46 wonderful years he spent night after night exploring every nook and cranny of my body."

Helen Slayton-Hughes as Ethel Beavers

Born in 1930, Helen Slayton-Hughes is the oldest cast member in *Parks and Recreation*. She manages to steal every scene as Ethel Beavers, court stenographer, who works on the notorious fourth floor of City Hall. Ethel does not smile, and her no-nonsense demeanor never changes, whether she is handing out a marriage certificate to newlyweds, taking notes in court or describing her steamy affair with Mayor Gunderson at his memorial service.

Slayton-Hughes has had many supporting roles in her television career, including in *That's So Raven*, *Arrested Development*, *Malcolm in the Middle* and *The West Wing*. Initially when shooting the Mayor Gunderson funeral episode, she was not aware who was playing the mayor, and initially had to act alongside an empty coffin. As she told *Entertainment Weekly*, "They explained to me that they couldn't shoot the whole scene until they knew he was available at the last minute. I was thrilled ... and then I got to be hugged by Bill Murray for a long, long time."

Fred Armisen as Raul

Raul visits Pawnee from the town's sister city in Venezuela. Raul is unimpressed with Pawnee and refuses to drink their tap water. He assumes that Tom is a servant, and Tom takes tips from him. Leslie initially tries to impress the delegation from Venezuela, hoping they will make a donation to turn the abandoned pit into a park. However, after bragging about their riches from selling oil and insulting the town and most of the people in the Parks Department, Leslie refuses his offer.

Fred Armisen, also a *Saturday Night Live* veteran, has had success in films including *Eurotrip* (2004) and *Anchorman* (2004). Along with Carrie Brownstein, Armisen created and starred in the sketch comedy series *Portlandia*, for which he has been nominated for an Emmy Award for Outstanding Writing for a Variety Series.

John McCain as Himself

When Leslie is in Washington visiting Ben, she becomes intimidated by the powerful connections he is making and begins to compare herself to them. She freaks out and takes refuge in a walk-in wardrobe, interrupted in the moment by John McCain, who she doesn't even turn around to face. When he tries to get his coat, Leslie asks him to leave and give her some privacy.

John McCain was a Republican politician and former presidential nominee who passed away in 2018.

Joe Biden as Himself

When Joe Biden appeared on *Parks and Recreation* he was revered as Barack Obama's vice president, a job he carried until 2017. He is frequently mentioned in episodes, especially relating to Leslie's crush on him. In Season 5, Ben arranges for Leslie to meet Biden as an engagement present. In Season 7, we find Leslie and Ben visiting Biden's house for a party.

Andy Samberg as Carl

Samberg appears as Carl, the park security guard who shouts instead of speaking, which he is oblivious to because he works outside all day. When interviewed about his role, Samberg stated, "Well, I don't want to jinx it, but I'm pretty sure it's the best episode, and maybe not just of this show but of any show on television ever, any theater show, any staged show, movie, or any, like, campfire ritual performed by cavemen. Take it all the way back. I think this is going to be the thing everyone talks about for the rest of their lives, and it will live on in infamy and history. If aliens came down and wanted one artefact to learn about human life, I think it would be this episode of *Parks and Recreation*. And you can take that to the bank."

Another *Saturday Night Live* alumnus, Andy Samberg is a member of the comedy music group The Lonely Island, along with two other of his *SNL* co-stars, and has been credited with popularizing *SNL* digital shorts. Samberg has appeared in the comedy films *I Love You, Man* (2009) and *Popstar: Never Stop Never Stopping* (2016). Since 2013, Samberg has produced and starred in the hugely successful sitcom *Brooklyn Nine-Nine*, for which he received a Golden Globe for Best Actor – Television Series Musical or Comedy in 2014.

Henry Winkler as Dr. Saperstein

Dr. Lu Saperstein is Pawnee's most famous obstetrician, a keen entrepreneur and the long-suffering father of the self-obsessed twin siblings, Jean-Ralphio and Mona-Lisa.

Henry Winkler has appeared in countless films and TV shows, but most notably graced our TV screens throughout the 70s and 80s as 1950s greaser and heart throb Arthur "Fonzie" Fonzarelli in *Happy Days*. Arguably one of the most popular sitcom characters of all time, Winkler won two Golden Globe awards for his role as The Fonz.

Megan Mullally as Tammy II

Tammy II, Ron's second and most powerful ex-wife, makes several appearances, breezing into his life to cause trouble and often to tempt him into sex in sleazy motels. Her power over Ron is so strong that she has convinced him to marry her, get his hair braided into corn rows, and have sex in a courthouse. Much of their chemistry can be attributed to the fact that Mullally is Nick Offerman's real-life partner. The couple have stated that they will do anything for comedy, which is particularly evident in Tammy's final appearance in *Parks and Recreation*, where she strips naked in a public library.

Mullally is most famous for her Broadway career and as Karen on *Will & Grace*, for which she received eight Emmy nominations, winning twice, in 2000 and 2006. Mullally and Offerman published their autobiographical book, *The Greatest Love Story Ever Told*, in 2018, which was a New York Times Bestseller.

HOSTING THE PERFECT
Galentine's Day

Every February 13th I like to celebrate Galentine's Day. It's kind of like Lilith Fair minus the angst and plus frittata. It's a lunch but with breakfast food. Some people might call this brunch, but it is so much more than that. It's a time for ladies to celebrate other ladies! On this day I celebrate all the amazing, beautiful women in my life. And the most beautiful of all is Ann.

I found my first Galentine's Day a bit intimidating, especially when Leslie presented me with her gift – hand-crocheted flower pens and a mosaic portrait of me made from the crushed bottles of my favorite diet soda. I thought that would be it, then Leslie presented me with a 5,000-word essay on why I am so awesome.

That's nothing compared to the needlepoint cushions I made last year with the ladies' faces on them, along with a newspaper headline from the day they were born.

I just don't know where to put that cushion right now, but I love it.

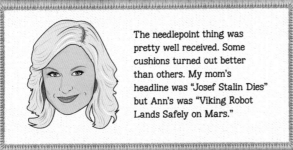

The needlepoint thing was pretty well received. Some cushions turned out better than others. My mom's headline was "Josef Stalin Dies" but Ann's was "Viking Robot Lands Safely on Mars."

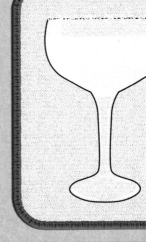

It's certainly a conversation starter. What I really love about Galentine's Day is catching up on all the things we have achieved in the past year. Except when I have a bad year. Though Leslie always has a way of making me feel good about myself.

Ann, you are a beautiful tropical fish. I truly believe that Galentine's Day should be made into a national holiday.

TOM: Donna and I are here to tell you about the best day of the year! Once a year, we take a day off and treat ourselves. And I don't mean just going to the spa and then the mall. When you wanna treat yo self, you still go to the spa and then the mall ... but in VIP style.

DONNA: I like to treat myself nice every day, because Donna Meagle is worth it. But this day is next-level nice.

TOM: We are talking top of the line EVERYTHING. Clothes, fragrances, massages, mimosas, fine leather goods. It's the one day of the year I allow myself to be selfish!

DONNA: We usually start out with valet parking. I do not street-park my Mercedes. Then we book in for some acupuncture therapy, before the beauty salon. My theory is, needles in your face, pleasure in your base!

TOM: After the salon comes the shopping. And nothing is off the table. When you treat yo self, there is no budget. There is no item too luxurious or outrageous. Crystal beetle brooch? Treat yo self. Four thousand thread count sheets? Treat yo self. Velvet slippies? Treat yo self.

DONNA: One time we took Ben with us when he was feeling down. It took him a while to get it, but by the end of the day he'd spent $1,900 on a Batman costume.

TOM: A couple years ago we went to Beverly Hills and ate sushi that was made from fish that were formerly owned by celebrities. Josh Groban was there eating his own sushi!

DONNA: Listen, my cousin is Ginuwine. I love him, but I didn't see any of his fish on the menu. Or his crabs.

TOM: Before that meal we got our elbows bedazzled, and fingernail Lasik. My nails haven't grown a millimeter since, and I still can't feel the ends of my fingies!

SEASON SEVEN

It is 2017, and we find Leslie trying to win a bid to turn a large pocket of formerly privately owned land in Pawnee into a national park. She is no longer friends with Ron, because of something called Morningstar, which occurred two years ago. The Gryzzl social media company has set up a headquarters in Pawnee. Andy has his own Johnny Karate TV show, with some of the Parks staff as recurring guests. Tom's Bistro is going well, and he now owns several restaurants. Ron has gone into private enterprise and started the Very Good Building & Development Co. Donna is getting married to Joe.

Jeremy Jamm is dating Tammy II and she is trying to turn him into Ron. Leslie enlists Ron to help Jamm escape from her, including deploying a metal chastity belt. Tom and Andy take a drunken cab ride to Chicago so Tom can reconnect with Lucy, five years after they dated. He invites her back to Pawnee to work at Tom's Bistro.

Tempers flare between Ron and Leslie. The team have had enough and come up with a scheme to get them to sort out their problems by locking them in the office at City Hall overnight. They finally discuss Morningstar. It is revealed to be a luxury apartment building Ron built on top of Ann's old house, next to Pawnee Commons, which has been built on Lot 58. Ron reveals that he left the Parks Department because Leslie stood him up for lunch at JJ's Diner, rushing to Washington instead. Ron was going to ask Leslie for a job in the federal government that day because he missed his friends. Ron and Leslie make up and end up drinking whiskey and changing the office back to the way it was when they worked together.

Gryzzl goes up against Leslie for possession of land that is owned by the Newport family. Leslie wants to turn the land into a national park and Gryzzl wants to use it for its new headquarters. It is revealed that Gryzzl has been spying on people's texts and emails.

Leslie debates the company on the TV show *The Perdples Court*. Jen wants Ben to run for the House of Representatives, but he doesn't know what to do. On a rare night without the kids, Ben and Leslie get drunk and call Jen to tell her Ben wants to do it. Donna's wedding goes off without a hitch, as she has deployed April to stop her family from causing a drama. Ben officially announces to the team that he is running for office.

April wants to leave her job but hasn't told Leslie. Leslie gives her a five-year plan binder for her job in government, increasing the pressure on her. Leslie gets offered a job in Washington and wants to take April with her. April admits that she doesn't want to work in government and Leslie agrees to support her. April decides she wants to work for the American Service Foundation in Washington.

It's Johnny Karate's final TV show, because he is moving to Washington. April feels bad about moving him away from the show that he loves. Mayor Gunderson dies and Ben needs to find an interim mayor. Tom decides to propose to Lucy with Leslie's assistance in the "outrageous pageantry" he desires. Jerry, now known by his real name, Garry, is made interim mayor.

TOP 10 EPISODES

Rock Show
(Season 1, Episode 6)

Most of the first season is not representative of the show that *Parks and Recreation* would later be, however "Rock Show" stands out as a hilarious episode that sets the scene for the brilliance that is yet to come. Andy's band is playing at a local bar, and the whole team are in attendance. Andy and Ann's relationship is struggling after it is revealed that Andy could have had his leg casts taken off two weeks previously but opted to keep them on so that Ann would continue to wait on him.

Leslie's mother sets Leslie up on a date with George, an elderly zoning official who, after a disastrous dinner, falls asleep at the show. Ron is dating his ex-wife Tammy II's sister. Andy dedicates a song to Ann, but she is not impressed. Mark and Leslie end up drinking together at the end of the show. She gets excited that there is a chance for them, not knowing that he has hit on Ann earlier. They grab beers to go ahead to the pit where

they laugh and talk about the future of the pit. This is the first episode that truly shows Leslie's vulnerability and likeability. It also demonstrates the fractures in Ann's and Leslie's love lives, with both of them pursuing men that are not good for them.

"The band has had a few different names over the years. When we started, we were Teddy Bear Suicide, but then we changed it to Mouse Rat. Then we were God Hates Figs, Department of Homeland Obscurity, Flames for Flames, Muscle Confusion, Nothing Rhymes with Orange, then Everything Rhymes with Orange, Punch Face Champions, Rad Wagon, Puppy Pendulum, Possum Pendulum, Penis Pendulum, Handrail Suicide, Angel Snack, Just the Tip, Threeskin ... [long pause] ... Oh, Jet Black Pope. We went back to Mouse Rat, and now we are Scarecrow Boat. God, when I hear myself say 'Scarecrow Boat' out loud I kinda hate it ..."

Ron and Tammy
(Season 2, Episode 8)

The Library Department have filed a claim for the abandoned lot so they can build a new branch. We meet Ron's ex-wife Tammy Swanson (Tammy II), Deputy Director of the Library Department, who Ron refers to as the "worst person in the world." Leslie visits Tammy who is initially sweet to her and agrees to withdraw the application. Tammy asks Ron to lunch, which results in a huge fight, then kissing, attempting to have sex on the table, then a frantic drive to the nearest motel. Leslie is concerned that Tammy is using Ron to get a hold of the lot in exchange for "more sex."

Ron realizes he is under Tammy II's spell and asks Leslie to help him to end it. Ron manages to escape from Tammy's clutches after taking a push pin to the forehead, and Leslie and Ron celebrate in the office. Tammy II, played by Nick Offerman's real-life wife Megan Mullally, will go on to be a favorite recurring character in the show, stealing every scene with her terrifying sexual power over Ron.

"On my deathbed, my final wish is to have my ex-wives rushed to my side so I can use my dying breath to tell them both to go to hell one last time. Would I get married again? Oh, absolutely. If you don't believe in love, what's the point of living?"

Hunting Trip
(Season 2, Episode 10)

The men of the Parks Department are planning their annual hunting trip and Leslie convinces Ron to invite the girls. April and Andy are left behind at the office and start to bond. Leslie insists on partnering up with Ron for the hunt. Ron is shot in the head but luckily it is a minor injury. Someone also shoots the window of Donna's Mercedes, but nobody will own up. Leslie takes the rap for shooting Ron; however, it turns out to be Tom.

While the hunting trip takes up most of the screen time of this episode, it is the chemistry that is forming between April and Andy as they waste time together in the empty office that makes this episode great, setting the scene for their relationship to come.

"I think this is gonna be a really good bonding experience with Ron. Guys love it when you can show them you're better than they are at something they love."

Flu Season
(Season 3, Episode 2)

It's flu season in Pawnee and several members of the parks team are in the local hospital, being cared for by Ann. Despite his extreme fitness, Chris gets sick and "can't stop pooping." Finally, Ann is exposed to his vulnerable side, which she secretly enjoys. Leslie refuses to admit that she is sick too, as she is focussed on making her presentation to the Pawnee Chamber of Commerce about the planned Harvest Festival.

Ben admits Leslie to the hospital, but she escapes and gives an almost flawless presentation. This is despite hallucinating that the wall and floor have changed places and imagining that she was wearing a tiara when she arrived. Leslie's scenes as she battles through her illness are hilarious. But crucially, this is the first time that Ben sees how driven and unflappable Leslie truly is, which sparks his growing feelings for her.

"Leslie, I typed your symptoms into the thing up here, and it says you could have 'network connectivity problems'."

The Fight
(Season 3, Episode 13)

Chris fires the Health Department Public Relations Director and Leslie suggests that Ann should interview for the role. Ann agrees, and in typical Leslie style she provides Ann with an overwhelming amount of reading material to prepare for it. Tom unveils his new alcoholic drink, "Snake Juice," at a local club, inviting the team along. Leslie finds Ann partying hard at the club when she should be studying for her interview, and they have a Snake Juice-fueled argument. Leslie criticizes Ann's dating life and Ann tells Leslie she is moving too slow with Ben. Leslie insults Ann when she tells her she feels she must keep Ann motivated or she would not go anywhere. They drunkenly declare that they will not work together.

As the Parks team negotiate their terrible hangovers the next day, Ben visits Ann and asks her to forgive Leslie. Ann is moved by this gesture and reveals that Leslie likes him. At the interview, Ann and Leslie apologize to each other and take turns to vomit into a wastebasket. The hangovers depicted in this episode are truly relatable to all of us, and the fight is a galvanizing moment in Ann and Leslie's friendship.

"Try a little Snake Juice. It's 140 proof, which means it's 70 percent alcohol. But don't worry, there's plenty of caffeine in it to keep you awake."

The Comeback Kid
(Season 4, Episode 11)

Ben has been out of work for three weeks, and Chris finds him at his house making terrible calzones. Ben eventually realizes how depressed he is after showing Chris a five-second claymation video that took three weeks to produce. He eventually accepts the offer to become Leslie's campaign manager.

Leslie's campaign is in tatters after her suspension, so they organize a rally at a local sports venue, supported by local basketball legend Pete Disellio. As it turns out, the basketball rink has been replaced with an ice rink, and the red carpet Tom has ordered only extends a short distance across the ice to a podium with no stairs. In some of the finest physical comedy shown in the show, the team slip and slide across the ice to the tune of "Get on Your Feet," Leslie's speech is a disaster and Pete Disellio slips and hits his head while trying to slam dunk on the ice.

Halloween Surprise
(Season 5, Episode 5)

It is Halloween, and Diane invites Ron trick or treating with her daughters. Diane is called away by work halfway through proceedings, and Ron does a terrible job of looking after the girls. Diane is upset and Ron declares that he is not ready for a family, ending their relationship. April and Andy convince Ron that he is making a mistake and he apologizes to Diane. They all then go trick or treating again, despite it being a week after Halloween.

Jen talks to Ben about his future and offers him another campaign manager job in Washington. In one of the funniest and most flatulent moments of the show, Jerry has a mild heart attack including a lot of flatulence. At the hospital, Jerry worries about the medical bills and Leslie arranges a garage sale to raise money for him. Meanwhile she realizes that she wants to make plans for her own future. In a beautiful moment, while viewing the house she planned to move into with Ben, he arrives and proposes, much to the delight of every *Parks and Recreation* fan.

"Leslie wanted to hire a contractor to build the stage. I don't want to paint with a broad brush here, but every single contractor in the world is a miserable, incompetent thief."

"I just want to hear the doctor say that Jerry had a fart attack! Is that too much to ask?"

Moving Up
(Season 6, Episodes 21 and 22)

In this two-part episode, we find the team in the lead-up to the Unity Concert. Leslie has taken a job in Chicago but is in San Francisco to speak at the National Parks Conference. She is dazzled by her experience, including bumping into Michelle Obama (the First Lady actually appearing in a cameo). She outlines her plans to merge Eagleton into Pawnee in only 12 months, which is laughed off by the audience.

San Francisco tech startup Gryzzl is giving away free wi-fi to select US cities, so Ben decides to pitch Pawnee to them. They decline, but after seeing the Gryzzl owners playing the board game he invented, *The Cones of Dunshire*, Ben challenges them to a duel. He wins, and they give him another shot at free wi-fi for Pawnee. The plan for the Unity Concert is to get 2,000 signatures in support of the Pawnee–Eagleton merger. The Unity Concert is a huge success, with Mouse Rat, Duke Silver and a 3D hologram of Li'l Sebastian concluding the show with "5,000 Candles in the Wind." The team congratulate Leslie, then take her to City Hall where they unveil a Pawnee Founders Day memorial monument with her name inscribed on the monument, as one of the founders.

After discussing her future with Ron, Leslie has a new plan. If she can't move Pawnee to Chicago, she'll have to move Chicago to Pawnee. A month later, we see Leslie ending her time as Deputy Director and moving upstairs to the third floor, to start her new job as National Parks Service's Midwest Regional Director. Jumping ahead three more years, we find that her plan to open the National Parks Regional Office for the Midwest Division in Pawnee has come true, and she has had triplets with Ben.

"Every time someone in Pawnee clicks through a slideshow of American Music Award red-carpet side-boob fails, they'll say, 'Thank you, Ben Wyatt'."

Leslie and Ron
(Season 7, Episode 4)

Leslie and Ron have been locked inside their old office in the Parks Department in an attempt to get them to reconcile, as their relationship has fallen apart. They both try to escape, but it's impossible. Ron chooses to sit in silence while Leslie pesters him to get him to talk. He eventually can't take any more of Leslie's pleading and agrees to speak with her for three minutes. Leslie has put together a whiteboard chart outlining the key events that may have contributed to their friendship ending, culminating in the infamous "Morningstar" incident. We learn that Morningstar was a luxury apartment complex that Ron's building company built on top of Ann's old house. Leslie was furious with Ron for this and stopped talking to him.

Just before the three minutes is up, Ron reveals that there is more to the story of what happened and why he left the Parks Department, and then escapes into his office. Ron tries to use the land mine on his desk to escape but finds that it is filled with confetti and a birthday message from Leslie, planted years ago. As negotiations continue, Ron tries pulling the fire switch. It simply causes the sprinklers to come on and drench them both. Ron finally tells Leslie the truth over a shared bottle of alcohol that Ron finds in a drawer. He explains that when Leslie left and took Jerry and April with her, Ron didn't know anyone in the department

anymore. When he decided to swallow his pride and ask Leslie for a job with her over lunch, she stood him up, deciding to travel to Washington for a last-minute work emergency. Ron was dejected and left to start his own building company and took on the Morningstar project.

By the next day, Ron and Leslie are happy to be friends again, despite their hangovers. The pair then head off to JJ's Diner to have "too much breakfast."

(Leslie trying to sing along to "We Didn't Start the Fire" by Billy Joel, without knowing the words): "Harry Truman was a guy. America. Red China. All the countries. Other people. Everyone is fun! Joe Mantegna, Ian McKellen. I have to buy a new toaster. This is awesome! You're so stupid! Jumping up and down. Whooo!"

LESLIE: The moment I met Ann, I knew I had found the woman that I would spend the rest of my life with. My best friend, soulmate and opalescent tree shark, the beautiful Ann Perkins.

ANN: When I met Leslie I knew I didn't really have a choice. But she is such an amazing person. Leslie is the kindest and most selfless friend. She even let me date Mark, a guy she used to have a crush on.

LESLIE: As I always say, ovaries before brovaries!

ANN: Gynecology before guy-necology!

LESLIE: I like to honor my friendship with Ann by celebrating all of our anniversaries. Like the first day we met. The first time we went out for breakfast at JJ's Diner. Talk Like a Pirate Day. Talk Like a Pittsburgh Pirate Day. I like to make scrapbooks of our memories together. Ours is a friendship so grand it truly takes 103 scrapbooks to capture.

ANN: Leslie gives the best dating advice. Just when I think things can't get any worse, she will tell me one of her dating disaster stories and all of a sudden I don't feel so bad.

LESLIE: Ann is right. I once got dumped by a guy while we were showering together. What about the time I went to a wedding where I used to go out with the groom? I was the only one there without a date, so the bride made me dance to "Single Ladies" by myself.

ANN: Before Leslie met Ben, I used to try to give her advice about men too. Sometimes she'd come to my place before a date to borrow an outfit. And I'd gently talk her out of wearing cargo pants.

LESLIE: Also Ann and I love exactly the same things! We have never disagreed on a single thing.

ANN: You did make me watch all eight Harry Potter movies. I don't even like Harry Potter.

LESLIE: That's insane! You love Harry Potter! You've seen all eight movies! We have so much in common. Some people think we are a couple when they meet us. The greatest tragedy in this world is that we are both heterosexual.

ANN: It would be a lot easier if we just became a couple in some ways. It would make it less weird when I wake up in the morning and Leslie is sleeping on my bed.

LESLIE: Oh Ann, you poetic and noble land-mermaid. I guess I'll talk to you later. And by that I mean I will text you 20–30 times tonight.

ANN, YOU CUNNING, PLIABLE, CHESTNUT-HAIRED SUNFISH.

Johnny Karate's Advice to Kids

Welcome to the only show that's all about learning, music, animals, fireworks, water skis and, above all, ice cream, pizza, ninjas, getting stronger, sharks vs. bears and, above all, karate! Today I want to talk to all of the kids that watch my show and talk about something that all of us feel sometimes ... our feelings! Feelings can be weird, and they come in all shapes and sizes.

If you are scared of the dark or thunder or spiders, that's OK! Everyone is scared of something. Follow my simple rules: Every day you should try to make something, learn something, karate chop something and try something new, even if it scares you! I once broke both my legs when I fell into a huge pit in the town. Boy was I scared when I had to go to the hospital. They had needles and scissors and it smelled a lot like pee in there most of the time. But then I got two awesome casts on my legs, all the Jello I could eat and the best part was – the pit got turned into a cool park!

But being scared isn't the only feeling you can feel. Sometimes we can feel sad too. Maybe you feel sad because someone at school farted in your lunch. Maybe your mom and dad had a fight, or you left your favorite candy bar on the bus. One time I lost my guitar. My guitar was worth over nine hundred million dollars! I cried all night. But when I woke up, my mom made me pancakes and took me to the video store. Suddenly everything felt better!

Have you ever done something you felt embarrassed about after? Man, it sure feels bad when you do. But don't worry, everyone in the world has done an embarrassing thing at least once. Some people have done a whole bunch of embarrassing things. We're all the same. Just remember though, the only way to fix doing an embarrassing thing is to do a good thing! Sometimes you've just gotta laugh it off or say sorry. And everybody pees the bed sometimes. It's what you do right after that counts.

And if you really don't know what to do sometimes, just take my advice – be nice to someone!

RON SWANSON'S

Love of Wood

Like any decent American man, I like to make things with my hands. And my preferred medium is wood, though I have been known to occasionally work with steel and once fashioned wedding rings out of a light fitting. I have been woodworking since a very young age. I made my first chair when I was five, but the wood was wanting. So, when I turned nine, I used my factory wages to purchase some beautiful local walnut.

I have a woodshop in my house. Sure, it doesn't exactly meet every building code. When people question me about this, I simply hand them my woodworking license. It's a piece of paper with "I can do what I want" written on it. I like to challenge myself with my woodwork. I even constructed a harp after drinking six whiskies to prove a point to Leslie. I make flutes too, however recently I have moved on to handcrafting canoes.

These skills come in handy in other areas of my life. Every two weeks I have to sand down my toenails. They are too strong for clippers. I own one wooden comb that I've had since I was six weeks old. When I look at men these days I am filled with horror. Most men are too focussed on their looks or their phones. These people don't understand the simple joy of a perfectly level jack plane. The satisfaction of wiping the sawdust out of your mustache and taking the first sip of whiskey after a long day sanding an oar that you crafted yourself. These boneheads have never woken up to the aroma of freshly varnished oak drying in the morning sun, while a naked woman sleeps peacefully beside them.

I plan to keep making things until the day I die. My final project will be building my own coffin. At the moment I'm leaning toward mahogany, but when the right tree finds me, I'll know.

MY ONLY OFFICIAL
RECOMMENDATIONS ARE
US ARMY-ISSUED MUSTACHE
TRIMMERS, MORTON'S SALT,
AND THE C.R. LAURENCE FEIN
TWO-INCH AXE-STYLE SCRAPER
OSCILLATING KNIFE BLADE.

Ask the Parks Department

I'm sixteen and thinking about getting my first tattoo using a fake ID. Should I do it and will it hurt?

LESLIE: Absolutely not! And of course it will hurt. That's it, get your mom on the phone. I want to talk to her.

APRIL: Totally, you should get one. The guy who works in the pawn shop can do it for you. He's not qualified but he's got a tattoo gun that someone traded in. Yeah, it's going to hurt. And it will bleed a lot, which is awesome. Anyway I think the guy has a pill bucket or something behind the counter and you can take whatever you want from it.

My parents are pressuring me to go to college, but I don't want to go. Should I tell them or just follow their wishes?

LESLIE: I encourage you to go to college and educate yourself. But more importantly, you should enroll as an intern at the Parks Department. Take a look at April and what it's done for her career.

RON: Listen to me and listen hard. There is nothing a college can teach someone that working in a sawmill can't.

APRIL: College sucks and being an intern is lame.

I'm a shy woman but I have met someone at work who I am interested in. How can I show my crush that I like them without making a fool of myself?

ANN: I don't know, I always just try to find a shared interest and talk to them about it. Or failing that, I tend to take on their interests and hobbies. Although sometimes I forget what my own interests are.

DONNA: Ann, did you grow up in the woods? Are you "Nell" from the movie *Nell*?. Girl, you need to start off with your outfit. He's not going to notice you if you keep shopping at the mall. All the good stuff is online. Give me your credit card and I'll show you.

TOM: Donna is right. Have you thought about using glitter in your makeup? What about your laundry powder?

I'm a 75-year-old woman and I enjoy making love with multiple partners at the retirement home. But how do I stay safe from diseases? I heard that half of the residents here have chlamydia.

RON: Good God, woman. Control yourself.

LESLIE: That's enough Ron. Everyone should be allowed to be sexual, no matter how gross it is to people like us.

ANN: The government says that abstinence is the best way to prevent the spread of sexually transmitted diseases. But we can't tell people to just stop having sex. We need to educate people about using protection so that they can still enjoy sex without the risk.

ANDY: But what if the sex is super gross?

RON: That's it, I am out of here.

LESLIE: Let me take you through the process of putting on a condom. I will demonstrate using this cucumber, grown here in good old Pawnee.

THE FINALE

The gang get together at the Parks Department office in the year 2017 to say goodbye to each other as their lives are about to take all of them in different directions. Spanning across two episodes "One Last Ride" takes us far into the future, giving us a glimpse into the lives of the Parks team.

Donna

2023: Donna and Joe are living a luxurious life in Seattle, where she is a successful real estate agent. She uses some of her commission money to create "Teach Yo Self," an education program with April, which helps struggling students with math.

Craig

2019: Craig has taken up a career in lounge singing at Tom's Bistro. He gets engaged to local hairdresser Typhoon. In the far future, we see an elderly Typhoon and Craig enjoying a submarine trip. Craig is still unhappy, on this occasion about the trout he has been served.

Jeremy Jamm

2022: Jamm is now a proud employee of a Benihana in Daytona Beach.

Tom

2022: Tom is married to Lucy. He is bankrupt after the stock market dried up and his restaurant suffered when the country ran out of beef. He achieves success with his book *Failure: An American Success Story*.

April and Andy

2022: Living in Washington, April and Andy are up to their old role-playing games as Burt Macklin and Janet Snakehole for Halloween. Andy wants to "put a baby" in April. Leslie gives April the advice that she and Andy are a good team, and that it might be time to add some more team members. As time moves forward, we then see April in labor, giving birth in Halloween makeup, while listening to "Monster Mash." The baby is named Jack (short for Burt Snakehole Ludgate Karate Dracula Macklin Demon Jack-o-Lantern Dwyer).

Jerry

2019: Jerry (Garry) has been officially elected after his interim term as mayor.
2048: He is voted in as mayor for the tenth time. He is 100 years old. He dies on his 100th birthday with his seemingly ageless family by his side. We see that his name is spelled wrong on the tombstone.

Jean-Ralphio

2022: We see Jean-Ralphio's funeral after he fakes his own death for the insurance money. His plot is revealed when he is exposed by the Rabbi at the burial while singing about starting a casino in Tajikistan with Mona-Lisa.

Ron

2022: Ron's company is still successful, however he resigns as chairman. His family is doing well and one of his children has been accepted at Stanford. He has diversified his portfolio and purchased 51 percent of a Scottish whiskey distillery. Leslie offers Ron the job of running the national park next to Pawnee, which was donated by Gryzzl. Even though he would be working for the federal government, Ron's nightmare, he accepts the job and sails off onto the lake in a wooden canoe, the appropriately named "Lucky Boy."

Ben and Leslie

2025: Ben and Leslie are at Joe Biden's house in Washington for dinner. Leslie is working for the interior and hears that the role of governor of Indiana is up for grabs. Ben is still a congressman, but Jen encourages him to run for governor of Indiana too. Ben and Leslie try to decide who should do it but decide to head back to Pawnee first.

The gang are back together in Pawnee for a reunion. Ann and Chris have two children and one is named Leslie. They are moving back to Pawnee and Chris will run admissions at the University of Indiana. Ben and Leslie decide to flip a coin to decide who will run for governor. Ben stops and decides that Leslie should run, and Ben will manage the campaign.

2035: At a speech at Indiana University, we find that Leslie has had two terms as governor. Leslie reflects on her time at the Parks Department as the team watch on as she is given an honorary doctorate. She encourages the crowd to go find their team and do their work. The Leslie Knope Library is named after her, much to her horror.

The final scene

In the last scene of *Parks and Recreation*, we say goodbye to the team as they pose for a group photo. Ben asks Leslie if she is ready for the picture to be taken. She takes one last look and replies "Yes, I'm ready."

The Paley Center for Media held the *Parks and Recreation 10th Anniversary Reunion* at PaleyFest in 2019, inviting the main cast, and Michael Schur, the creator and show runner. Amy Poehler was visibly emotional throughout the reunion and described herself as "totally overwhelmed." She referred to Leslie Knope as "the Spiderman of public service," who might be of benefit in the current political climate in America, which is so far from where it was in 2009.

During the reunion the cast reflect on how "Galentine's Day" and "Treat Yo Self" have become part of popular culture and are now appropriated by brands. Aziz Ansari draws a parallel between Tom and Jean-Ralphio's money-making schemes to the recent Fyre Festival financial collapse, which went viral around the world, insisting that Tom and Jean-Ralphio "would have gotten Ja Rule." When discussing the USA College admission scandal of 2019, Ansari tells the crowd "that's some Eagleton shit."

Schur describes *Parks and Recreation* as a show about female friendship. Rashida Jones agrees, adding, "Things like Leslie thinking Ann is the best, smartest, most beautiful, naïve, rule-breaking moth. There is something so tender and sweet about that to me because in some regards Ann, she's alright, she's cool, she's good, she's doing her best, but Leslie just fucking loves her so much and she just bolsters her as a human being."

Schur also reveals that the day after the show ended the set was being demolished. Nick Offerman salvaged all the oak doors from the set and made the cast canoe paddles with the seal of Pawnee on them. When asked about the possibility of *Parks and Recreation* returning to our screens in some way, Schur said, "Everything comes back and is cycled through again. Everyone on this stage would have to feel like there was a story that needed to be told ... The show had an argument to be made. And the argument was about teamwork and friendship and positivity and being an optimist and not getting cynical and believing that people could be good ... I don't feel like we left anything on the table. The show made its argument."

Though the show finished in 2009, its exposure on Netflix has led to the *Parks and Recreation* fandom getting bigger as time goes by. In addition to streaming, fans are able to enjoy endless YouTube compilations of bloopers from the show, including Chris Pratt's hilarious farting and ad-libbing.

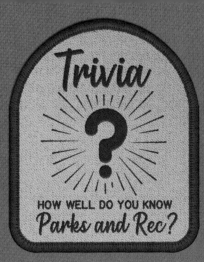

Trivia

?

HOW WELL DO YOU KNOW
Parks and Rec?

1
What is Donna's spirit dog?

2
What is Ben's sexual fetish?

3
What is Ron Swanson's middle name?

4
How many eggs did Ron eat to break the record at JJ's Diner?

5
Where was Tom born?

6
What is written on the land mine on Ron's desk?

7
What is Joan Callamezzo's favorite cocktail?

8
Who is Leslie's celebrity crush?

9
What is the name of the Pawnee resident who scored a last-second dunk in 1992 at a basketball game against Eagleton High?

10
What is Andy's favorite football team?

11
What is Donna Meagle's favorite city?

12
Where does April go during the government shutdown?

13
Who does Joan Callamezzo want to perform at her "Walk of Fame" ceremony?

14
How many nicknames does Garry Gergich have?

15
Where does Tom work during the government shut down?

16
What is the Lot number of the Pawnee pit?

17
What kind of car does Donna drive?

18
What is Tom's shoe size?

19
What is the name of Jerry's dog?

20
Which famous sports star is Ron's post-sex outfit based on?

Answers

1 A cat

2 Women on roller skates

3 Ulysses

4 51

5 South Carolina

6 Front Towards Enemy

7 A tumbler of gin with crushed aspirin around the rim

8 Joe Biden

9 "Pistol" Pete Disiello

10 The Indianapolis Colts

11 Seattle

12 Venezuela

13 Buddy Holly

14 Four: Jerry, Larry, Terry and Lenny

15 Lady Foot Locker

16 48

17 Mercedes Benz

18 6¾

19 Lord Sheldon

20 Tiger Woods

Smith Street Books

Published in 2020 by Smith Street Books
Naarm | Melbourne | Australia
smithstreetbooks.com

ISBN: 978-1-92581-146-9

Publisher: Paul McNally
Project editor: Hannah Koelmeyer
Editor: Ariana Klepac
Design and layout: Stephanie Spartels
Illustrations: Chantel de Sousa, The Illustration Room
Proofreader: Pam Dunne

Printed & bound in China by C&C Offset Printing Co., Ltd.

Book 122
10 9 8 7 6 5 4 3 2 1